This Coloring Book belongs to

. . . .

Coloring Book

Hokusai

Prestel

Munich · London · New York

'My oh my, this man really has got a lot of wrinkles!'

That is surely what you first think when you see the drawing of this old man. It shows the Japanese painter, Hokusai, who was born in 1760 and became famous through his color woodblock prints. Crafting pictures using woodblocks is quite a complicated art form: to begin with, a flat image is carved from a panel of wood; next, the raised bits are colored in and pressed onto a sheet of paper; and then you see the colored outlines. And for every colored space, an individual printing plate has to be created.

Although Hokusai painted a whole range of different images, he was always fascinated by particular topics. Among these was the sacred Mount Fuji, which was the highest mountain in Japan and still an active volcano. He painted it from 36 perspectives. Don't you think that the pictures make good postcards?
Can you find Mount Fuji on them?

'The Great Wave of Kanagawa' (cover illustration) is part of the series: '36 Views of Mount Fuji'. This is probably Hokusai's best known woodblock color print. And in the background you can find Mount Fuji. The great wave however is going to carry you off on an exciting journey to Japan. Are you ready?

This is your ship and this is where you begin your big journey. So what are you taking with you to Japan?

Up till now, the sea was very calm. But suddenly a storm is brewing up and a wave rises.
It is dragging you to the other side of the world.
Can you paint some fish, whales and other creatures of the ocean?

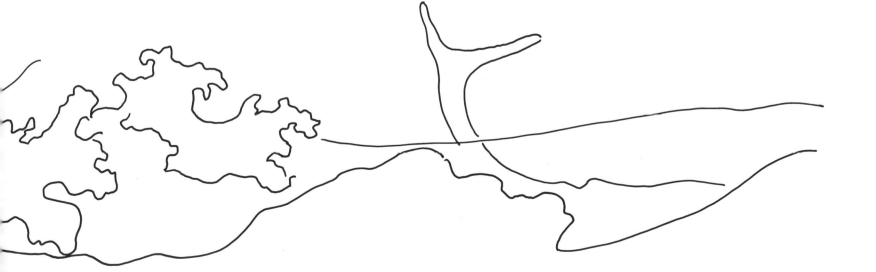

The sea has settled down again. The Japanese guests on board have gathered at the barrier and are looking forward to their homeland. What does Japan look like?

What has this stylish lady discovered through her telescope?
Perhaps it's the snow-covered peak of Mount Fuji?

You could go ashore in this beautiful bay.

And would you like a cup of tea?

You could paint your very own Japanese postcard right here.

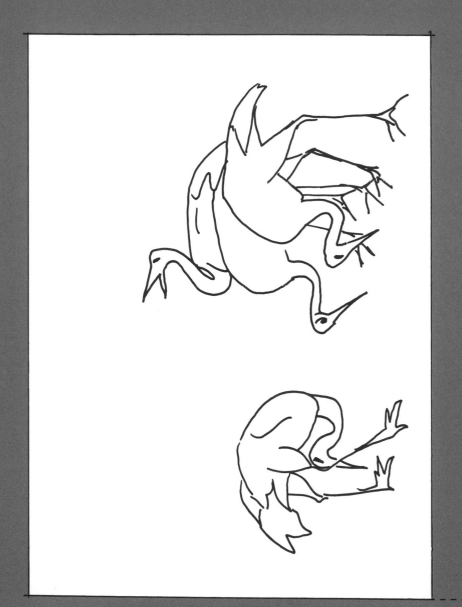

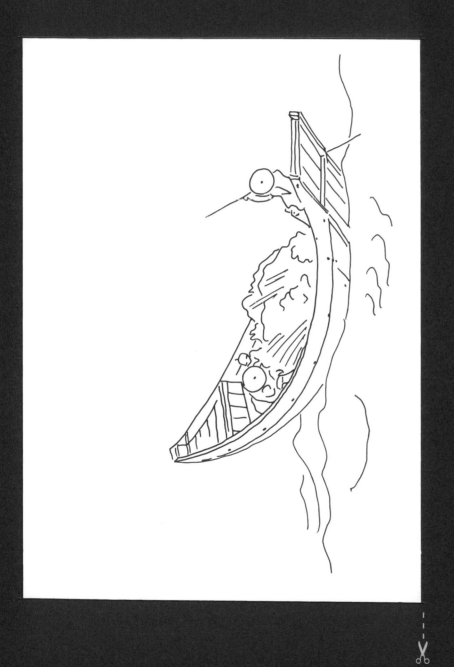

In Japan, writing is a grand art form. Why not try to copy these words:

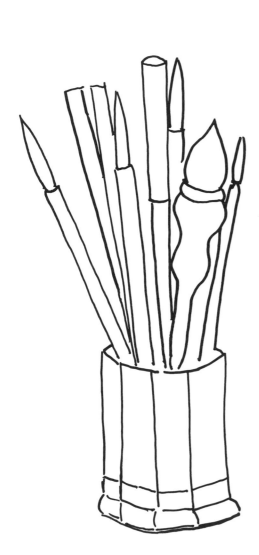

Horse

うま

Boat

ふね

Water

みず

Hop on a horse and gallop away to really get to know the country.
What does the countryside you are riding through look like?

These fine ladies are wearing very pretty clothes. Are there flowers on the material?

But these figures look a little bit terrifying? Might be an idea to ride a bit quicker! Don't worry, they are only actors.

You can stay overnight in this little hut.
Can you make out Mount Fuji in the distance?

You can set off in a little boat next morning and get off at a new embankment ...

These bearers are carrying goods to the next village.

Where is this bridge leading to and what can you see below it?

It's time to go home now. There is a ship in this bay. But a whale is also stranded there!

You've only just boarded and your ship and the whale are being snatched by the enormous wave and carried out to the open sea. We are returning to your homeland now …

The original pictures of Hokusai.

Here you will find a few pictures that have been used as blueprints for this book. Which ones do you recognize?

Because many of the pictures Hokusai made were prints, many different copies of his colored works are scattered all over the world. Here we are showing you some museums, where you will definitely be able to find these prints.

The actor Sakata Hangorō III as a travelling priest, actually Chinzei Hachirō Tametomo, Photo: British Museum, London
The actor Ichikawa Ebizo as Sanzoku, actually Mongaku Shōnin, 1791. Photo: Museum of Fine Arts, Boston, William Sturgis Bigelow Collection.

Woman with a Telescope. From the series: *The Seven Bad Habits*, approx. 1800–02. Hagi Prefectural Art Museum.

Lady with a fan and a lady holding an insect keepsake box, approx. 1810–12. Idemitsu Museum of Arts, Tokyo.

Teapot, porcelain jug and earthenware mug decorated with Sōma Horses / Sōma Pieces. From the series: *A Set of Horses*, 1822. Rijksprentenkabinet, Rijksmuseum, Amsterdam.

Ink pot and pot with brush / Obsidian. From the series: *A Set of Horses*, 1822. Photo: Museum of Asian Art, SMB, Berlin.

Pink Lilies on a Blue Background. From the series: *Large Flowers*, 1832. Guimet Museum, Paris.

Orange Orchids. From the series: *Large Flowers*, 1832. Guimet Museum, Paris.

The Great Wave. From the series: *36 Views of Mount Fuji*, 1830–1836. The Metropolitan M of Art, New York. Photo: Artothek.

The River Tama in Musashi Province. From the series: *36 Views of Mount Fuji*, 1830–1836. Sumida Arts Foundation, Tokyo.

Tsukada Island in Musashi Province / Cushion Pine Trees at Aoyama. From the series: *36 Views of Mount Fuji*, 1830–1836. Private Collection.

South Wind, Clear Sky. From the series: *36 Views of Mount Fuji*, 1830–1836. Private Collection. Photo: Artothek

Tsukudajima in Musashi Province. From the series: *36 Views of Mount Fuji*, 1830–1836. Honolulu Academy of Arts.

Kajikazawa in Kai Province. From the series: *36 Views of Mount Fuji*, 1830–1836. Private Collection. Photo: Bridgeman Images.

Sazai Hall - 500 Rakan Temples. From the series: *36 Views of Mount Fuji*, 1830–1836. National Museum of Ethnology, Leiden.

Reflection in Lake Misaka, Kai Province. From the series: *36 Views of Mount Fuji*, 1830–1836. Minneapolis Institute of Arts. Photo: Bequest of Richard P. Gale / Bridgeman Images.

Sekiya Village on the Sumida River. From the series: *36 Views of Mount Fuji*, 1830–1836. State Pushkin Museum of Fine Arts, Moscow. Photo: Bridgeman Images.

Lake Suwa in Shinano Province. From the series: *36 Views of Mount Fuji*, 1830–1836. State Pushkin Museum of Fine Arts, Moscow.

At Sea off Kazusa. From the series: *36 Views of Mount Fuji*, 1830–1836. State Pushkin Museum of Fine Arts, Moscow.

Umezawa Village in Sagami Province. From the series: *36 Views of Mount Fuji*, 1830–1836. Minneapolis Institute of Arts. Photo: Bequest of Richard P. Gale / Bridgeman Images.

The Suspension Bridge on the Border of Hida und Etchu Provinces. From the series: *Remarkable Views of Bridges in Various Provinces*, approx. 1833. The Mann Collection, Highland Park, Illinois.

Whaling off Goto Island. From the series: *Oceans of Wisdom*, 1834. Photo: Bridgeman Images.

Self-portrait, approx. 1845–49. Guimet Museum, Paris.

© 2015, 3rd printing 2018,
Prestel Verlag, Munich · London · New York
A member of Verlagsgruppe Random House GmbH
Neumarkter Strasse 28 · 81673 Munich

Prestel Publishing Ltd.
14-17 Wells Street
London W1T 3PD

Prestel Publishing
900 Broadway, Suite 603
New York, NY 10003

Concept, drawings, and text: Maria Krause

Translation and copyediting: Paul Kelly
Design and layout: Meike Sellier, Eching
Production: Astrid Wedemeyer
Separations: ReproLine mediateam, Munich
Printing and Binding: Lanarepro GmbH, Lana
Paper: Tauro

MIX
Paper from
responsible sources
FSC® C016410

Verlagsgruppe Random House FSC® N001967

Printed in Italy

ISBN 978-3-7913-7215-0

www.prestel.com